First Facts®

Your Favorite Authors

Barbara Park

by Molly Kolpin

CAPSTONE PRESS
a capstone imprint

First Facts are published by Capstone Press,
1710 Roe Crest Drive, North Mankato, Minnesota 56003
www.capstonepub.com

Library of Congress Cataloging-in-Publication Data
Kolpin, Molly.
  Barbara Park / by Molly Kolpin.
      pages cm.—(First Facts. Your Favorite Authors)
  Includes bibliographical references and index.
  Summary: "Presents the life and career of Barbara Park, including her childhood, education,
and milestones as a best-selling children's author"—Provided by publisher.
  ISBN 978-1-4765-0223-6 (library binding)
  ISBN 978-1-4765-3438-1 (paperback)
  ISBN 978-1-4765-3420-6 (eBook PDF)
  1. Park, Barbara—Juvenile literature. 2. Authors, American—20th century—Biography—
Juvenile literature. 3. Children's stories—Authorship—Juvenile literature. I. Title.
  PS3566.A6725Z73 2014
  813'.54—dc23
  [B]   2013003116

Editorial Credits
Christopher L. Harbo, editor; Tracy Davies McCabe and Gene Bentdahl, designers;
Marcie Spence, media researcher; Kathy McColley, production specialist

Photo Credits
Alamy Images: Jeff Greenberg, 9 (middle), Mira, 7, ZUMA Wire Service, 19; Capstone:
Michael Byers, cover, 15 (bottom); Capstone Studio: Karon Dubke, 13 (top); Corbis: Stephanie
Kuykendal, 17; Courtesy of Barbara Park, 5 (bottom), 6, 21; Newscom: Charles Trainor Jr./
KRT, 11; Shutterstock: Ardelean Andreea, 9 (top and bottom), blue67design, design element,
Dario Sabljak, 13 (bottom), Filaphoto, 5 (top), malinx, design element, Pixsooz, 15 (top)

Printed in the United States of America in North Mankato, Minnesota.
032013   007223CGF13

Table of Contents

Chapter 1: A Call of a Lifetime

Barbara Park tried for months to get her first book published. Then one phone call changed her life. An **editor** told Barbara she would **publish** her first book, *Operation: Dump the Chump*. Park was thrilled. She had no idea a long and successful writing career was in her future.

---

editor—someone who checks the content of a book and gets it ready to be published

publish—to produce and distribute a book, magazine, or newspaper so that people can buy it

"Imagining the kind of success I've had would have been to imagine yourself winning the lottery."
—Barbara Park

Barbara Park with her dog, Maggie

Chapter 2: Finding Her Way

Barbara Park was born April 21, 1947, to Doris and Brooke Tidswell. She grew up in the small town of Mount Holly, New Jersey. When not tattling on her older brother, Barbara enjoyed reading comic books. At that time she hoped to someday become a teacher.

Barbara and her brother, Brooke

Wittiest of the Class

In high school Barbara was voted "wittiest" in her grade. She admits it wasn't as good as being voted "most likely to succeed." But she says, "it planted the seed that I might be able to write humor."

Mount Holly, New Jersey

Barbara started college at Rider University in New Jersey in 1965. Two years later she transferred to the University of Alabama. She studied education. She earned her degree, but she decided not to become a teacher.

Barbara married after graduating from college. She and her husband had two boys and moved to Arizona. Caring for her family was her full-time job. But when her sons started school she began feeling **restless**.

---

restless—when someone finds it hard to keep still or to concentrate on anything

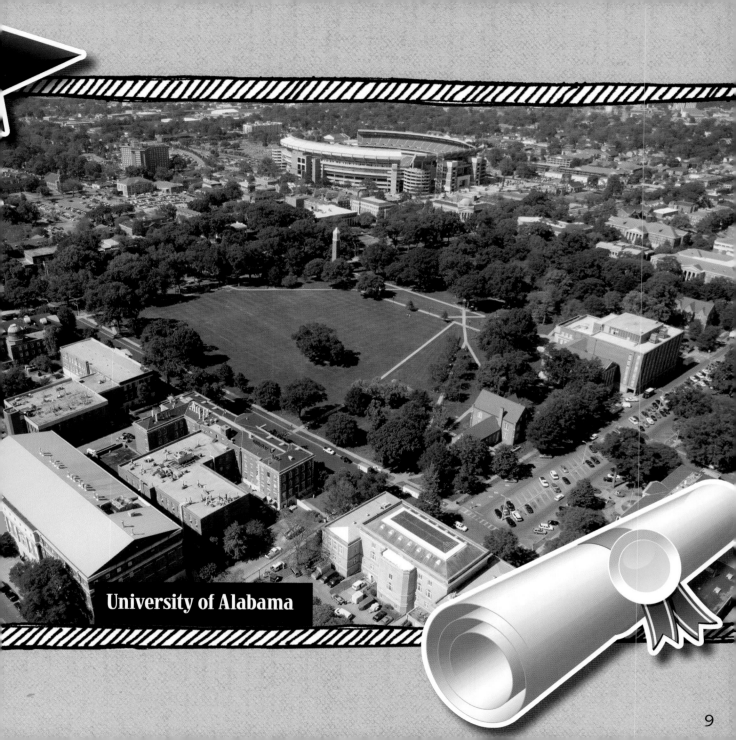

University of Alabama

In the late 1970s, Park had an idea. She decided to use her **comedic** talents as a writer. But newspapers and magazines **rejected** most of her early writing.

Then Park's son told her to read Judy Blume's *Tales of a Fourth Grade Nothing*. That's when Park realized she should become a children's author.

---

comedic—relating to comedy or humor
reject—to refuse to accept something

author Judy Blume

Chapter 3: A Storyteller Is Born

Park spent months writing her first book, *Operation: Dump the Chump*. Three publishing companies rejected the story. Finally it was accepted along with **manuscripts** for *Don't Make Me Smile* and *Skinnybones*. Of the three books, *Don't Make Me Smile* hit bookstores first in 1981.

---

manuscript—an author's original text for a story

Working in Pajamas

Park loves that being a writer means she can work in her pajamas. But that doesn't mean she's lazy about her job. Her work routine involves answering e-mails in the morning. Then she writes until dinnertime.

Park is known for being a funny author. But she has a serious side too. *Mick Harte Was Here* is about a boy who died in a biking accident. In *The Graduation of Jake Moon*, Park writes about **Alzheimer's disease**. Her ability to mix humor with serious topics is proof of her writing talents.

Alzheimer's disease—a disease that causes loss of memory, thinking, and language skills, and changes in behavior

"I have always enjoyed the rewriting and fine-tuning process. Polishing a manuscript is absolutely the best part of the process for me."—Barbara Park

Readers love the humor and **characters** in Park's stories. Her most popular character is 5-year-old Junie B. Jones. Park created Junie after being asked to write books for younger readers. Her first Junie book was *Junie B. Jones and the Stupid Smelly Bus*. It was an instant success.

---

character—a person or creature in a story

From 1992 through 2001, Park wrote 17 books about Junie's kindergarten adventures. She now writes about Junie's experiences in first grade. Junie's adventures in and out of school have made millions of readers laugh. More than 40 million Junie books have been sold.

Children watch a play starring the Junie B. Jones character at a museum in Albuquerque, New Mexico.

Chapter 4: A Successful Career

With more than 40 books and 40 awards, Park has had a busy career. Someday, though, she plans to spend less time writing. The good news is Park's characters will live on after she retires. And her stories will continue to make readers laugh for lifetimes to come.

"My goal was to establish myself as a well-respected, popular-selling children's author."
—Barbara Park

Timeline

1947	born April 21 in Mount Holly, New Jersey
1965	graduates from high school
1969	graduates from the University of Alabama; marries her college sweetheart, Richard Park
1981	*Don't Make Me Smile* is published
1982	*Operation: Dump the Chump* and *Skinnybones* are published
1992	*Junie B. Jones and the Stupid Smelly Bus* is published; it is the first of 17 Junie B. books set in kindergarten
1995	*Mick Harte Was Here* is published
2000	*The Graduation of Jake Moon* is published
2001	Junie enters first grade in *Junie B., First Grader (at last!)*
2009	*Junie B.'s Essential Survival Guide to School* is published
2012	*Junie B., First Grader: Turkeys We Have Loved and Eaten (and Other Thankful Stuff)* is published; it is the 28th Junie B. book to be published
2013	continues to write and live with her husband in Arizona

Glossary

Alzheimer's disease (AHLTS-hahy-merz dih-ZEEZ)—a disease that causes loss of memory, thinking, and language skills, and changes in behavior

character (KAR-ik-ter)—a person or creature in a story

comedic (kuh-MEE-dik)—relating to comedy or humor

editor (ED-uh-tur)—someone who checks the content of a book and gets it ready to be published

manuscript (MAN-yuh-skript)—an author's original text for a story

publish (PUHB-lish)—to produce and distribute a book, magazine, or newspaper so that people can buy it

reject (ri-JEKT)—to refuse to accept something, such as an idea, drawing, or book

restless (REST-liss)—when someone finds it hard to keep still or to concentrate on anything

Read More

Fandel, Jennifer. *You Can Write Awesome Stories*. You Can Write. North Mankato, Minn.: Capstone Press, 2012.

Llanas, Sheila Griffin. *Picture Yourself Writing Fiction: Using Photos to Inspire Writing*. See It, Write It. Mankato, Minn.: Capstone Press, 2012.

Index

Internet Sites

FactHound offers a safe, fun way to find Internet sites related to this book. All of the sites on FactHound have been researched by our staff.

Here's all you do:

Visit *www.facthound.com*

Type in this code: 9781476502236

Super-cool stuff!

Check out projects, games and lots more at
www.capstonekids.com